THE *Flowers* COLOURING & CRAFT BOOK

LISA HUGHES

ILLUSTRATED BY
PATRICIA MOFFETT

CARLTON
BOOKS

THIS IS A CARLTON BOOK

Published by Carlton Books Ltd
20 Mortimer Street
London W1T 3JW

Copyright © Carlton Publishing
Group 2016

A CIP catalogue for this book is
available from the British Library.

Project editor: Charlotte Selby
Design manager: Lucy Palmer
Layout: Rebecca Wright
Production: Ebyan Egal

ISBN 978-1-78097-817-8

Printed in China

10 9 8 7 6 5 4 3 2

INTRODUCTION

If, like me, you really enjoy colouring and crafting, you'll love this book, because it combines them both! The projects are all fun and easy to make, and they feature a selection of lovely floral patterns. What's particularly exciting is that the results will be really special and completely unique, because they'll be handmade by you.

To get started you'll need colouring pens, pencils or paints, and scissors. Any other materials that are required are listed, but they're items you're likely to have around anyway or you can improvise. If you only need to colour one side of a piece, the instructions will say so and you can choose which side to colour. Otherwise, colour both sides. If you'd rather not cut the book up, you can also photocopy, scan or trace the designs, as long as it's only for your personal use.

Being creative is an ideal way of de-stressing and can greatly improve our sense of well-being, so I really hope you find making these projects pleasurable and rewarding.

Lisa Hughes

THE PALETTES

Here are some colour combinations to inspire your craft projects.

PALETTE N°·1
A
B
C
D

PALETTE N°·5
A
B
C
D

PALETTE N°·9
A
B
C
D

PALETTE N°·13
A
B
C
D

PALETTE N°·17
A
B
C
D

PALETTE N°·2
A
B
C
D

PALETTE N°·6
A
B
C
D

PALETTE N°·10
A
B
C
D

PALETTE N°·14
A
B
C
D

PALETTE N°·18
A
B
C
D

PALETTE N°·3
A
B
C
D

PALETTE N°·7
A
B
C
D

PALETTE N°·11
A
B
C
D

PALETTE N°·15
A
B
C
D

PALETTE N°·19
A
B
C
D

PALETTE N°·4
A
B
C
D

PALETTE N°·8
A
B
C
D

PALETTE N°·12
A
B
C
D

PALETTE N°·16
A
B
C
D

PALETTE N°·20
A
B
C
D

CONTENTS

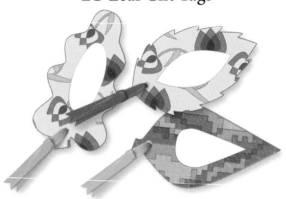

THE PATTERNS

THE PROJECTS

Thank You Card Toppers

Giving flowers is a universal way of thanking someone – for a present, an invitation or simply being a good friend. These flower toppers are ideal for decorating thank you cards, but can be used for any message or occasion.

MATERIALS AND TOOLS

- A6 card blank or card
- Glue or double-sided sticky tape

INSTRUCTIONS

1 Choose the toppers you want to use, colour them in – you only need to colour one side – and cut them out.

2 Take a card blank – if you're creating your own, measure to fit the envelope, cut and fold the card – and play around with the toppers until you have an arrangement that you like.

3 Stick the toppers to the card.

MORE IDEAS AND INFORMATION

• You can embellish the front of your card with small buttons, bows, ribbon, washi tape or a handwritten message.

• To create a 3D effect, raise the toppers above the card by using double-sided sticky pads.

• Adding a couple of the smaller flowers to the inside of the card is a nice touch, too.

Pop-up Gift Card Holder

Gift cards are a great solution for people who are difficult to buy for, but they're not very personal and their presentation often leaves a lot to be desired. This gift card holder is a lovely way to address that.

MATERIALS AND TOOLS

- Medium-thick card 10cm x 18cm
- Glue or double-sided sticky tape
- Bone folder
- Metal ruler

INSTRUCTIONS

1 On the large pieces, colour one side of the rectangular areas, but both sides of the flap. On the band, colour both sides. Cut them all out.

2 Stick the paper without the flap to one side of the card (this is the inside).

Stick the paper with the flap to the other side, leaving the flap hanging (this is the outside).

3 Using a bone folder and a metal ruler, score two lines on the inside and one on the outside as marked, and fold the card to form a V shape on the outside.

4 On the outside, run a 0.5cm wide strip of double-sided sticky tape along the top edge of one half of the V and press the V firmly together.

5 Turn over and cut out the blank area of the part that stands up as marked. Place the gift card in this pocket.

6 Close the card, fold over the flap, wrap the band around it and tape the ends together.

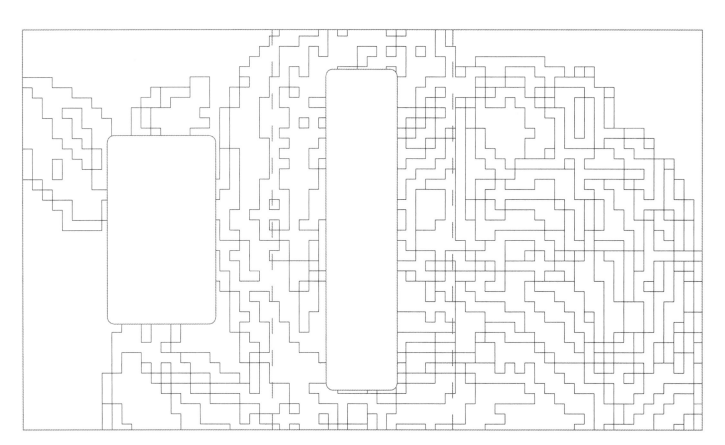

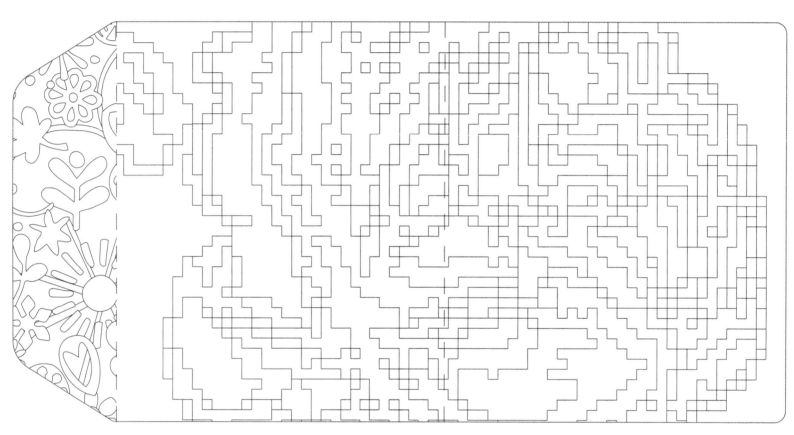

MORE IDEAS AND INFORMATION

- Write your message in the blank area and slip the gift card holder into a C7 envelope.

- Instead of a gift card, you could give money or a homemade 'voucher' for babysitting or decorating services.

- You could tie the holder closed with a ribbon, rather than the band.

Leaf Gift Tags

If you've spent time choosing a present, it's worth taking care with the finishing touches. The organic shapes of these gift tags give them a slightly rustic feel, but the patterns – and the colours you choose – will create quite a bold contrast.

MATERIALS AND TOOLS

- Hole punch
- Narrow ribbon

INSTRUCTIONS

1 Choose a gift tag. Colour it in and cut it out.

2 Punch a hole as marked. Double up a length of ribbon, thread the loop through the hole, take the loose ends up and through the loop, and tighten gently.

3 Write your message and attach to your gift. The process is the same for all the gift tags.

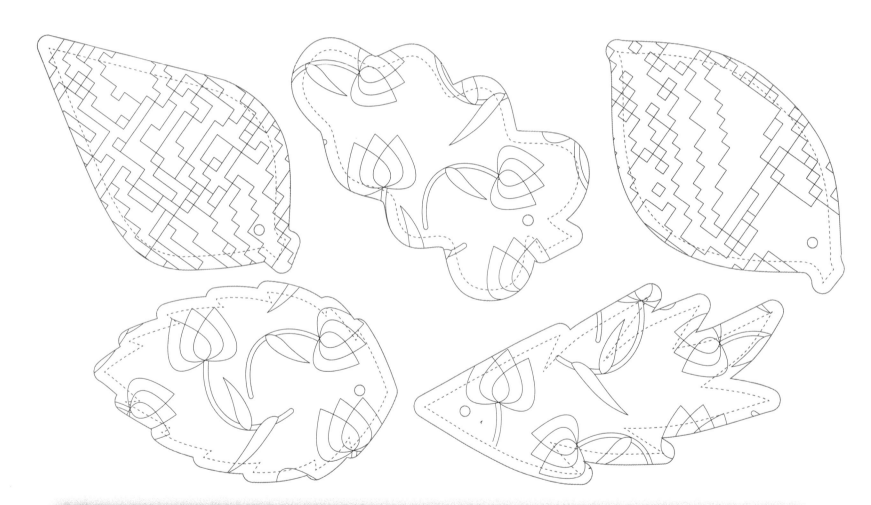

MORE IDEAS AND INFORMATION

• Fresh shades of spring green or warm autumn colours are the obvious choices, but don't be limited by realism!

• These tags can be used to label anything, particularly if you laminate them so that they'll last.

• You could also colour just one side and make a small collage with them.

Fruit and Veg Fridge Magnets

Scribbled shopping lists, bills waiting to be paid, takeaway menus, children's art – fridge magnets are incredibly handy for keeping important paperwork in order. Here you can make your own stylish set, custom-coloured to complement your kitchen decor.

MATERIALS AND TOOLS

- Medium-thick card
- Magnetic sheet
- Glue or double-sided sticky tape

INSTRUCTIONS

1 Choose the magnets you want to make, colour them in – you only need to colour one side – and cut them out.

2 Mount them on the card, then on the magnetic sheet, and cut them out again.

MORE IDEAS AND INFORMATION

- Disc or block magnets give a stronger hold than magnetic sheet.

- If your fridge door isn't accessible, you could paint an area of the kitchen wall or a noticeboard with magnetic paint.

- These fruit and veg shapes could also be used to decorate a recipe binder.

Cake Stand

Of course this cake stand won't last forever – it's made of paper! – but it will hold chocolates, biscuits and even cupcakes, as long as your baking isn't too heavy-handed. What's more, it's fun to put together and looks absolutely charming.

MATERIALS AND TOOLS

- 1 paper plate about 18cm in diameter
- 1 paper plate about 22cm in diameter
- Glue or double-sided sticky tape and a glue gun
- Hole-maker
- A chopstick about 25cm long
- Two pieces of fairly stiff card, 5cm x 30cm and 5cm x 10cm

INSTRUCTIONS

1 Colour the circles, triangles and small double ring – you only need to colour one side – and cut them out.

2 Stick a circle to the top and bottom of the smaller plate and the top of the larger plate. If necessary, trim the circles or cut in from the edge so that they lie flat.

3 Trim the triangles and stick them around the top rims of both plates.

4 Make holes in the centres of the plates and push the chopstick through, leaving about 5cm sticking out at the bottom and about 15cm between the plates. Use the glue gun to hold them in place.

5 Bend the longer card strip into a circle and stick the ends together. Rest the stand on it and use the glue gun to hold it in place.

6 Stick the double ring to the other piece of card, cut it out, fold it in half and glue it around the top of the chopstick.

MORE IDEAS AND INFORMATION

• Make sure all edibles are wrapped or use food-safe craft varnish, which will make your stand last longer, too.

• This stand would be very useful for displaying small items at a craft fair.

• Cake stands don't have to be round – cut the paper plates into flower shapes or hexagons.

Jasmine-scented Garland

The slender, pure white petals of this garland hide delicate patterns, which you can colour in subtle or bold hues, and which are suddenly revealed when it moves. You can even add a perfume to really bring the outdoors in.

MATERIALS AND TOOLS

- Needle and 1.5m cotton thread
- White fabric scented with jasmine essential oil, cut into 1cm x 1cm squares
- Glue or glue gun

INSTRUCTIONS

1 Colour the patterned side of the flower shapes and cut them out.

2 With the patterned side upwards, crease the petals as marked, folding them inwards, then use a pencil to curl the bottom of each petal outwards. Repeat for all the flowers.

3 Thread the needle and tie a knot. Sew through a scented fabric square, then up through the patterned centre of a flower. Repeat for all the flowers. Spread them out at irregular intervals, leaving enough thread for hanging.

4 To hold the flowers in place on the thread, dab glue on the fabric, inside the flower and on top of the flower.

MORE IDEAS AND INFORMATION

- The obvious occasion to display this beautiful garland is at a wedding.

- A used tumble dryer sheet will take the essential oil well; alternatively scent the garland with room spray.

- To make more garlands, use the flower shape as a template and add your own patterns inside.

Birdhouse Bonbonniere

A bonbonniere is a small ornamental container designed to hold bonbons or sweets and often given as a gift. This one comes in the shape of a delightful birdhouse and it makes the perfect home for confectionery or chocolates.

MATERIALS AND TOOLS

- Craft knife and cutting surface
- Bone folder and metal ruler
- Double-sided sticky tape or glue

INSTRUCTIONS

1 Colour the pieces and cut them out, including the hole in the box door. Score along the dotted lines using the bone folder and metal ruler.

2 On the larger piece, the box bottom is surrounded by squares on three sides.

Take the smaller piece (without scalloping). With the blank sides facing down, stick the tabless end to the tab on the box bottom.

3 Fold up the attached piece and the piece opposite the door. Stick them together with the tabs.

The rest of the attached piece will form the roof.

4 Fold the piece without the hole up and the top of the box down. Stick them together with the tabs. You should have a cube with an opening door.

5 Take the rest of the attached piece over the box top – it should form an inverted V – and stick it to the outside top of the opposite side of the box with the tab.

6 Centre the scalloped piece over the roof and stick it down. Close the door.

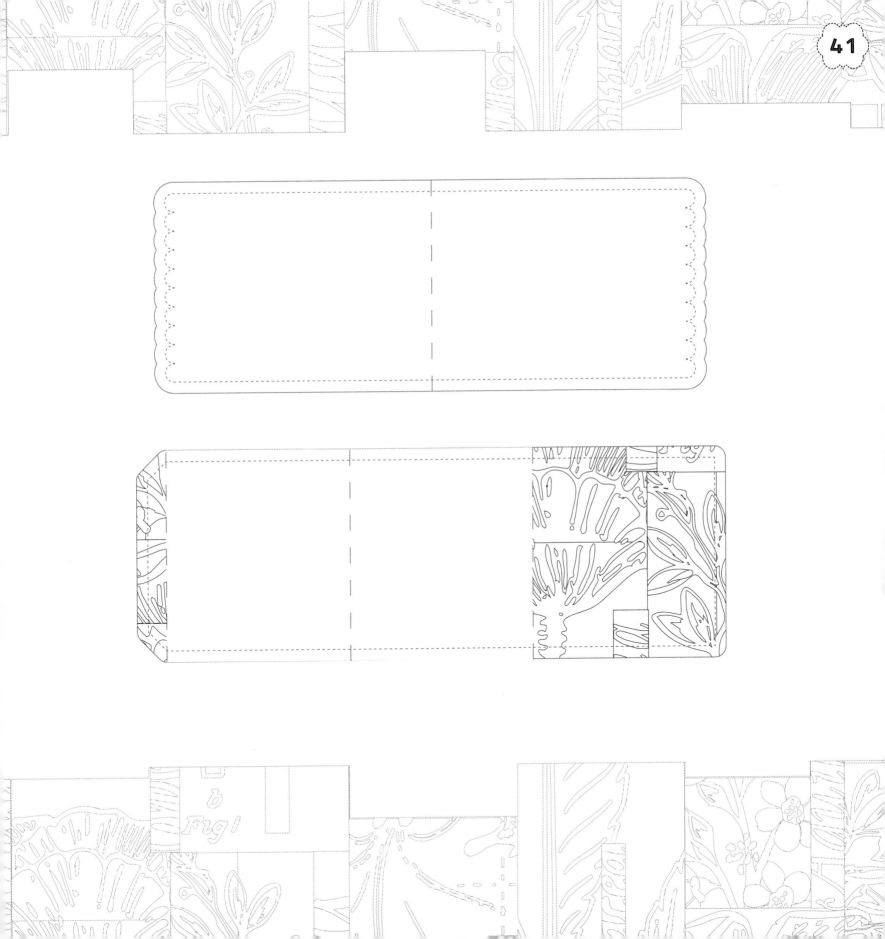

Fig 1

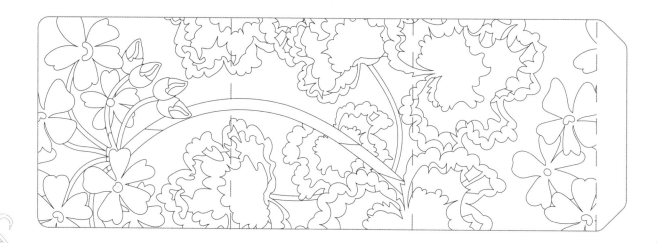

MORE IDEAS AND INFORMATION

- Fill with delicious sweets!

- To turn this bird box into a hanging ornament, make a ribbon hole in the centre of the scalloped piece before you stick it down.

- It would also be fun to make a small paper bird to live in the bird box.

Butterfly Picture

A flock, a flight or a flutter of butterflies are winging their way across this stunning artwork. The colouring and cutting require a little patience, but the effort is well worth it, because the resulting picture has real impact.

MATERIALS AND TOOLS

- Craft knife and cutting surface
- Low-tack tape
- A4 backing paper in white or a pale colour
- Glue or double-sided sticky tape

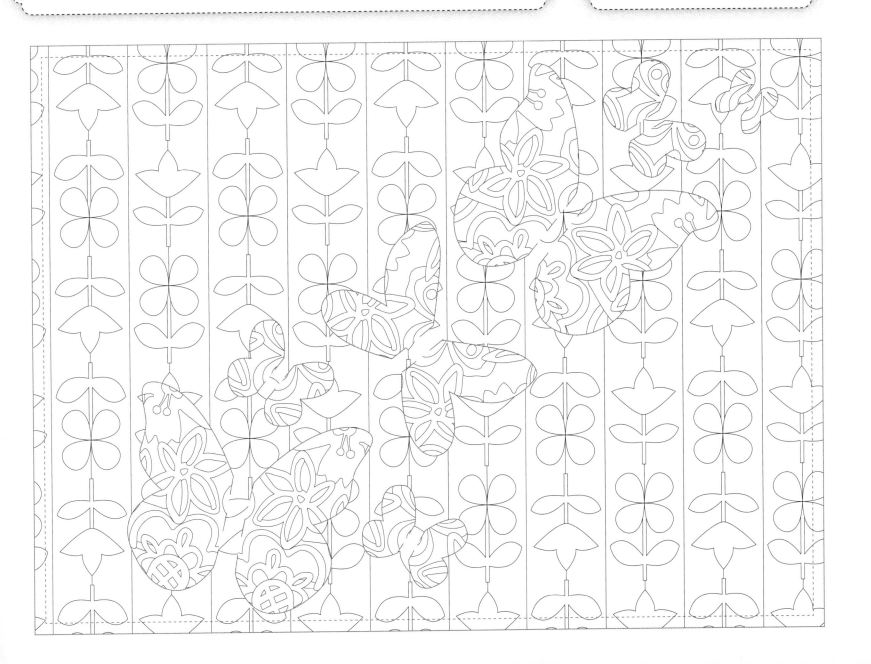

INSTRUCTIONS

1 Colour in all three pieces and cut out the rectangles.

2 Take the bottom section, with the three slightly larger small butterflies. With the fully patterned side facing up, tape it to your cutting surface to stop it slipping. Cut along the butterfly wing lines, remembering that you should never cut towards your other hand. For smooth lines, make a series of short cuts, rather than one long one, and move the paper, rather than the craft knife, round. Repeat for the top and middle sections.

3 From the back, gently loosen the wing shapes and push them forwards. Turn over and make sharp creases along the marked fold lines, so that the wings stand up.

4 Assemble the sections on the backing paper so that the butterflies form a diagonal line and stick them down.

MORE IDEAS AND INFORMATION

• Display this picture in an A4 box frame or just back it with card and prop it on a shelf.

• If you're not confident about paper-cutting, simply colour in the butterflies to make them stand out from the pattern.

• This technique also looks fantastic used on a card.

Daisy Headband

The humble daisy is a symbol of innocence, but it's also a cheerful flower that looks fun and fresh adorning a headband. This project is certainly simple to make and – have no doubt – heads will turn when you wear it!

MATERIALS AND TOOLS

- Thin card
- Glue or double-sided sticky tape

INSTRUCTIONS

1 Colour the two parts of the band, the daisies and the leaves – you only need to colour one side – and cut them out.

2 Mount the two parts of the band on the card, cut them out again and join them to form one long strip. Measure around your head, trimming or adding extra card if necessary.

3 Lay the band flat and arrange the daisies and leaves along it. Overlap the decorations, but don't hide the pattern on the band completely.

4 Join the ends of the band to form a circle.

MORE IDEAS AND INFORMATION

• This headband would obviously look charming on a little girl, but it could also be worn to a festival, an Easter parade or a '70s fancy dress party.

• If you have a left-over daisy, punch two holes in it and thread it onto a piece of ribbon for a matching necklace.

You can also use these flowers for card toppers or gift decorations.

Hanging Hot Air Balloon

Imagine how it would feel to float off in this sweet model of a hot air balloon... Sadly it's unlikely to take your weight, but the act of colouring it will be intensely calming and you'll find your cares just drift away!

MATERIALS AND TOOLS

- Glue or double-sided sticky tape
- Brown paper, 3cm x 10cm
- Four lengths of baker's twine, 7cm long
- Needle and thread

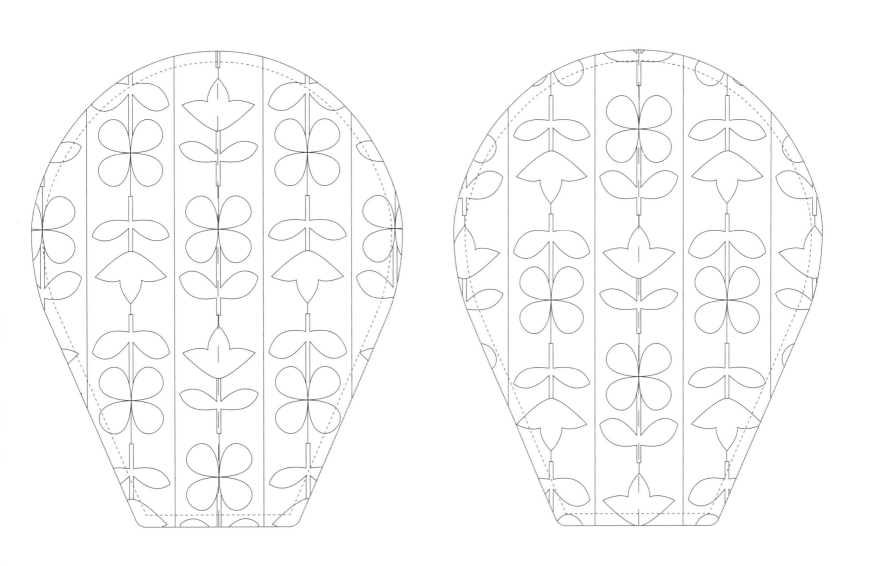

INSTRUCTIONS

1 Colour the balloons – you only need to colour one side – and cut them out. With the coloured-in sides inside, fold them in half as marked.

2 Stack the folded balloons together and stick each uncoloured side to the next one, but leave the bottom outer edge open for the basket strings.

3 Join the short ends of the brown paper to make a tube. This is the basket.

4 Stick the four 7cm lengths of baker's twine to the inside of the tube. These are the balloon strings and it's important they are evenly spaced and the same length.

5 Making sure they all stay the same length and hang straight, stick the strings 1cm in from the bottom outer edge of the balloon.

Stick the balloon's bottom corners together and open it out carefully.

6 Using the needle and thread, sew through the top of the balloon to make a loop for hanging.

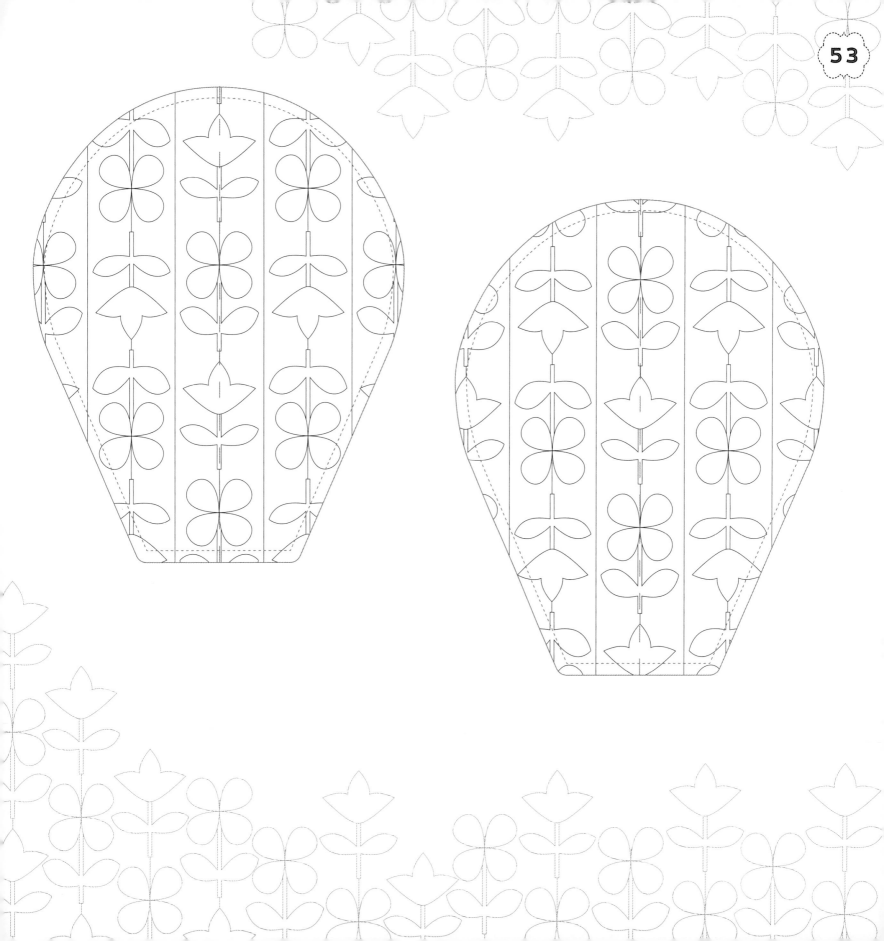

MORE IDEAS AND INFORMATION

• This would look delightful in a child's bedroom or a nursery, suspended above a cot.

• You could make tiny silhouette figures and stick them to the inside of the basket.

• Use card for the basket and straws – snip the ends to flatten them – for the strings if you want the balloon to stand rather than hang.

Paper-cut Frame Picture

When you've put time and effort into colouring a picture – and here you have a choice of two very intricate patterns – it deserves to be displayed. This project includes a frame, cut into the design, which will set off your work beautifully.

MATERIALS AND TOOLS

- Craft knife, cutting surface and metal ruler
- Low-tack tape
- A4 backing paper to complement the pattern colours
- Glue or double-sided sticky tape

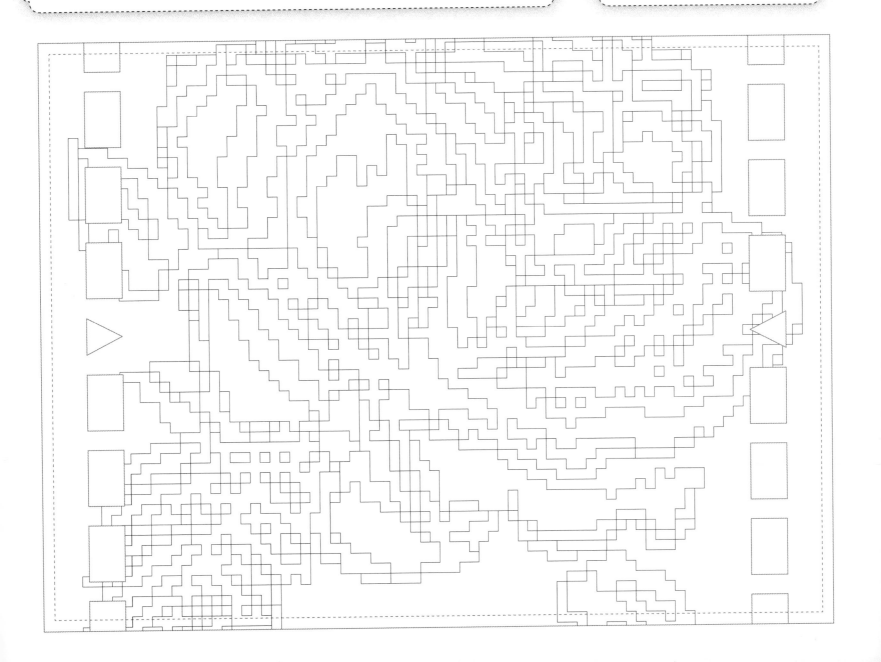

INSTRUCTIONS

1 Colour in all three pieces – you only need to colour one side and don't colour the blank areas. Cut out the rectangles.

2 Take the larger, middle section and tape it to your cutting surface to stop it slipping. Make the cuts as marked and press out the loose paper. It may be easier to move the paper around, rather than the craft knife. Repeat for the top and bottom sections.

3 Assemble the sections on the backing paper and stick them down.

MORE IDEAS AND INFORMATION

- If don't want to cut out the frame, simply colour it in – a really strong solid colour will work well.

- You could mix the central section from one pattern with the top and bottom from the other.

- If you use an A4 frame as well, pick one that is the same colour as the backing paper.

Grape Hyacinths

Artificial blooms are becoming more and more fashionable. This is partly because they can be enjoyed all year round and that's certainly true for these sweet paper ones, which do a passable imitation of the lovely spring flower, grape hyacinths.

MATERIALS AND TOOLS

- Strips of green tissue paper, 1cm wide
- Invisible tape or glue
- 3 chopsticks or straws, about 20cm long

INSTRUCTIONS

1 To make one flower, colour one narrow, one medium and one wide strip and cut them out.

2 Fold each strip in half lengthways. Leaving 0.5cm at each end, from the folded edge, make a series of cuts just less than 0.5cm apart, stopping about 0.5cm before the opposite edge.

3 To make the stem, stick a tissue paper strip to one end of a chopstick or straw and wind the tissue round it, moving down with each turn but avoiding gaps. Stick the end of the tissue down and use more strips if necessary.

4 Take the narrow patterned strip and stick it to the stem top. Wind it round the stem, positioning each layer under the one above. Do the same with the medium strip and then the wide strip.

5 With the end of a pencil, open out the loops in the paper. Make the other two flowers in the same way.

MORE IDEAS AND INFORMATION

- Before wrapping them, cut the chopsticks or straws to slightly different lengths and arrange the finished flowers in a bud vase.

- A shortened version could be pinned to a dress for a nice corsage.

- You don't have to use green tissue paper – the stems can be any colour you want.

Vase Sleeve

A simple, clear-glass vessel can be a lovely way of displaying flowers, but if you fancy a change and want to inject some bold pattern and colour into an arrangement, why not try making this clever vase sleeve?

MATERIALS AND TOOLS

- Craft knife and cutting surface
- Invisible tape
- Clear, straight-sided glass vase, about 8cm in diameter and 20cm tall

INSTRUCTIONS

1 Colour the two panels – you only need to colour one side – and cut out the rectangles.

2 Using the craft knife on your cutting surface, cut out the vase shape as marked.

Make sure you don't cut right across the shape at the top or bottom. This is the front of the sleeve.

3 With the patterns facing outwards, tape one long side of the front piece to one long side of the back piece. Do the same with the other sides. The aim is to create a tube that fits round the vase fairly snugly, so adjust as necessary. If the sleeve is too tall, trim at the top rather than the bottom, but don't trim through the cut-out.

4 Slip the sleeve over the vase and gently pull the cut-out shape forward, so that it stands away from the vase. Fill with flowers.

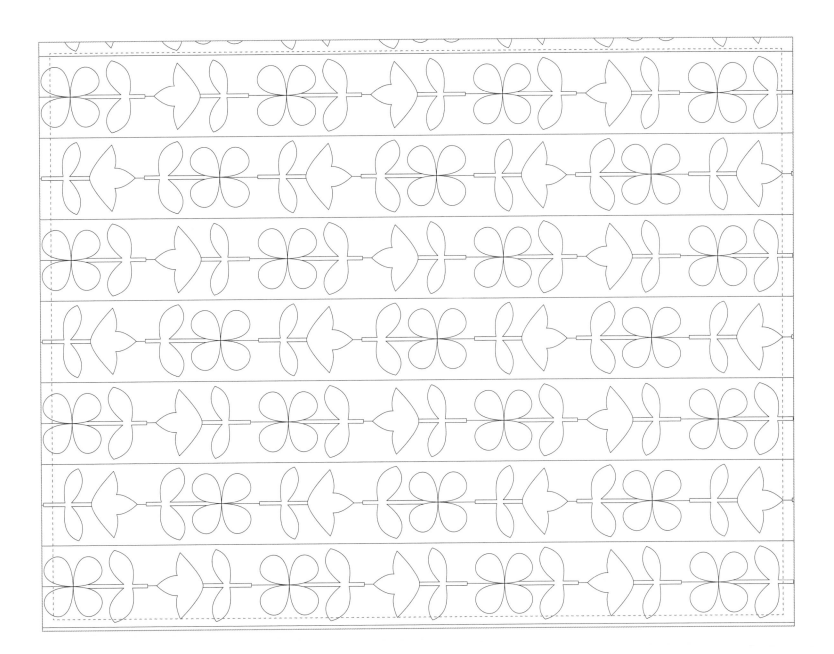

MORE IDEAS AND INFORMATION

- Extend this for a larger diameter vase by adding extra paper where the pieces join.

- You may glimpse the inside of the sleeve, so colour both sides of the pieces if you want to.

- You could also wrap a plain paper sleeve around the vase and put the sleeve over the top.

Decoupaged Craft Supplies Container

An organised workspace is a happy workspace – fact! And whether it's a place for pens or paperclips, if you colour and craft your own storage solutions you'll be even happier. Plus anyone who hasn't tried decoupage before will find it's quite addictive!

MATERIALS AND TOOLS

- Small, clean container – for example, a jar, takeaway coffee cup, yoghurt pot or small tin
- Glue
- Gloss varnish and brush

INSTRUCTIONS

1 Colour the decoupage strips – you only need to colour one side – and cut them out. For a very small container, you may not need them all.

2 Glue the strips to the outside of the container in whatever arrangement you choose. Smooth out any wrinkles and let the glue dry.

3 Give the container at least three coats of varnish – the more, the better. Let the varnish dry between coats, be careful not to seal in any dust and sand lightly between coats if there are any lumps or bumps.

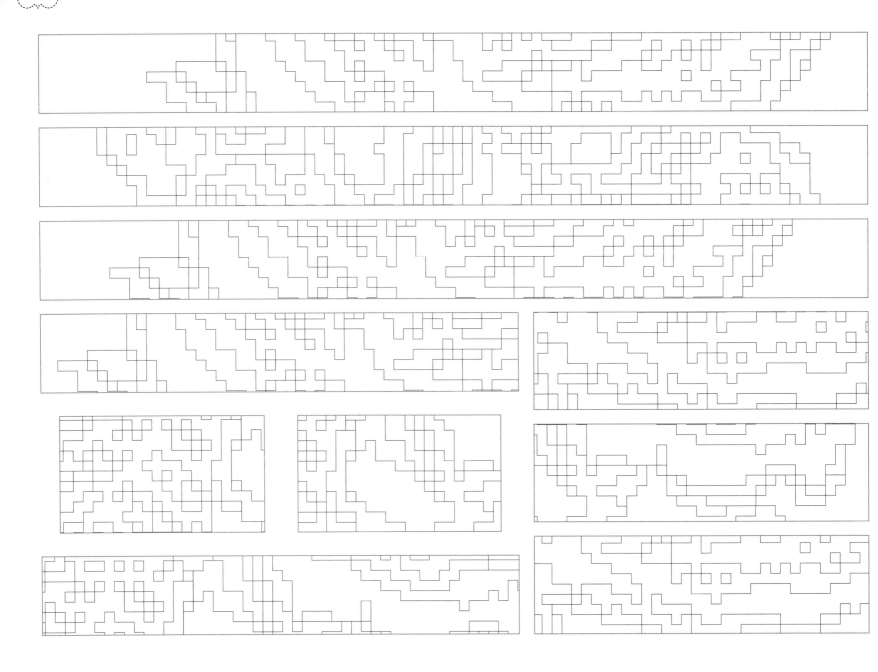

MORE IDEAS AND INFORMATION

• Storage boxes, drawers, files – anything you keep craft supplies in is a great opportunity for decoupage.

• Gloss varnish doesn't cloud no matter how many layers you use, but for a matt finish put matt varnish on as the final layer.

• If you don't have varnish, PVA glue is a good substitute, but you'll still need several coats.

Seed Packets

Seeds gathered from your own garden make the ideal gift for a fellow gardener, and these hand-coloured seed packets are the perfect way of presenting them. Needless to say, you can also use them yourself for storing seed until it's time to plant.

MATERIALS AND TOOLS

- Bone folder and metal ruler
- Glue or double-sided sticky tape

INSTRUCTIONS

1 Colour a front, a back and a small circle – you only need to colour one side – and cut them out.

2 Using the bone folder and metal ruler, score the fold lines as marked.

3 Place the back on top of the front, patterns facing out. Fold the side and bottom tabs over the back and stick them down.

4 Write the type of seed and date collected in the empty space. To close, slip the top flap inside the packet and seal by sticking a circle over the top edge.

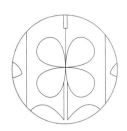

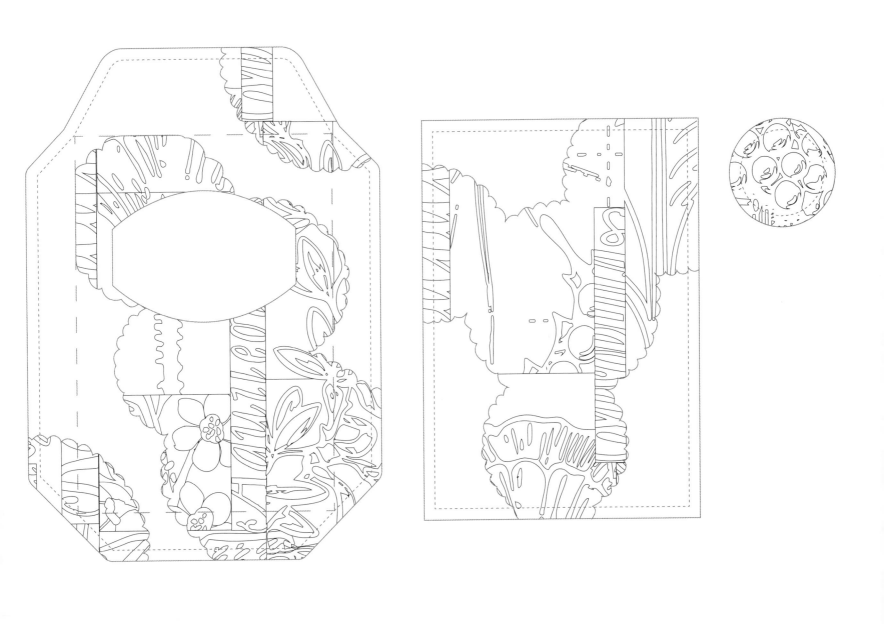

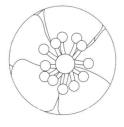

MORE IDEAS AND INFORMATION

• These packets can be used for notes or small homemade cards, too – your card should be slightly smaller than 7cm x 10cm.

• They are also a good place for keeping buttons or scraps of ribbon and lace for crafting.

• Or pin the packet to your noticeboard through the open flap and keep business cards in it.

Bookmarks

So many people read on electronic devices, but when you come to read a book it's special and you should keep your place with something equally special and personal to you. Here you'll find three different bookmarks to colour and craft.

MATERIALS AND TOOLS

- Bone folder or blunt knife
- Metal ruler
- Glue or double-sided sticky tape
- Hole punch
- Narrow ribbon

INSTRUCTIONS

1 To make one corner bookmark, colour one piece as marked and cut it out. Score the lines as marked. With the two triangles pointing up and the blank one on the left, fold down the right triangle. Fold the left one on top of it and stick them together. This fits over the corner of the page you're reading.

2 To make a long, thin bookmark, colour it and cut it out. Punch a hole as marked. Fold the ribbon in half and thread the loop end through the hole from front to back. Bring the loose ends over the top, thread them through the loop and gently pull to tighten.

3 To make an arrow bookmark, colour one large and three small arrows and cut them out. Punch holes as marked. Place the three smaller arrows on top of the large one and link them together with ribbon.

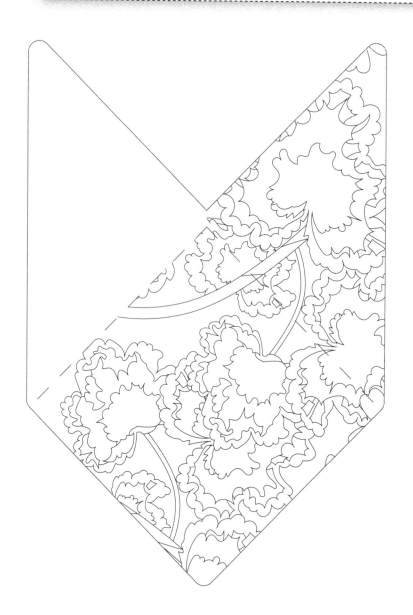

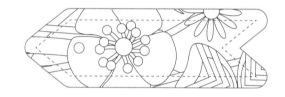

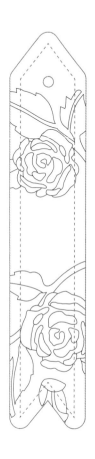

MORE IDEAS AND INFORMATION

• When you give someone a book, give them a homemade bookmark, too.

• You could decorate any of these bookmarks with washi tape or a small initial.

• Turn the corner bookmark into a monster by inserting a zig-zag of white paper teeth between the two triangles and adding eyes to the top section.

Noughts and Crosses

It's a time-honoured way of passing the time, and, yes, you can have a game with paper and pen – but how much more pleasing to play with a rather nice set of noughts and crosses that you've coloured and made yourself!

MATERIALS AND TOOLS

- Medium-thick card
- Glue or double-sided sticky tape

INSTRUCTIONS

1 Colour the board and cards – you only need to colour one side – and cut them out.

2 Mount on the card and cut them out again.

3 To play, two players take it in turns to place one of their cards on the board. The aim is to achieve a horizontal, vertical or diagonal line of three. The first one to do so, wins.

MORE IDEAS AND INFORMATION

- Pop the cards in an envelope – you could make one using the technique on page 71 – and take the set with you when you travel.

- Print nine small portraits from a special occasion and mount them on the board, one in each square.

- Send kisses and hugs with a prop-up picture – arrange four cards on a plain background to say 'XOXO'.

Boat Picture

Stylised boats, their sails adorned with captivating pattern, bob gently across this pretty picture. A joy to colour and craft, even if you're not a sea-going type, this idyllic and unique seascape will look fetching on any wall in your home.

MATERIALS AND TOOLS

- A4 backing paper in blue
- Glue or double-sided sticky tape

INSTRUCTIONS

1 Colour in all the pieces – you only need to colour one side – but make sure the circle contrasts with the rectangle. Cut out them out.

2 Take the backing paper and lay out the pieces. Place the large rectangle (the sky) across the top and the circle (the sun) on one side of it.

3 Place the triangle with the concave edge (the shore) in the opposite bottom corner and the boats on the blue area (the sea).

4 Once you're happy with the arrangement, stick the pieces down.

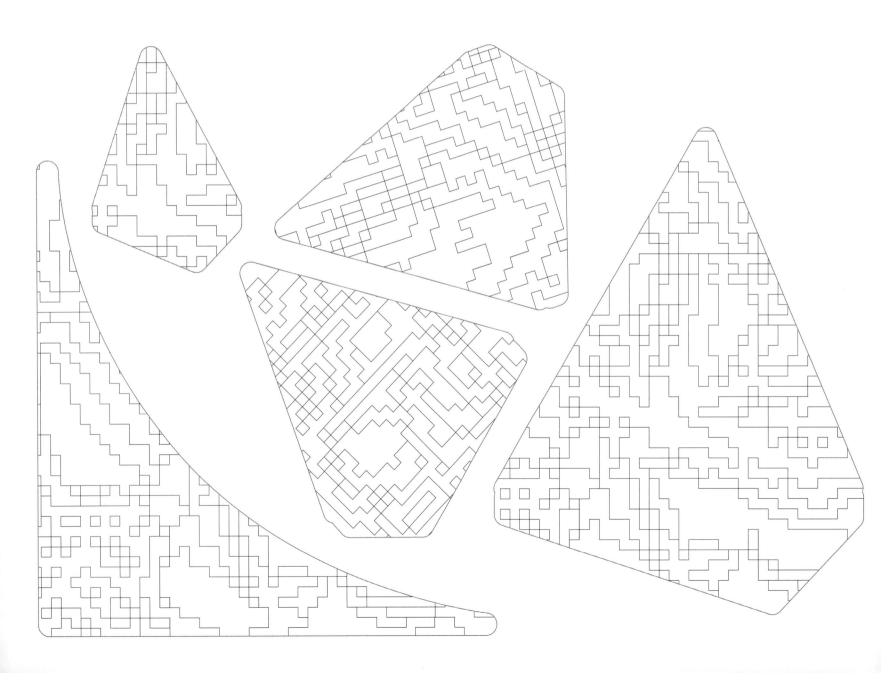

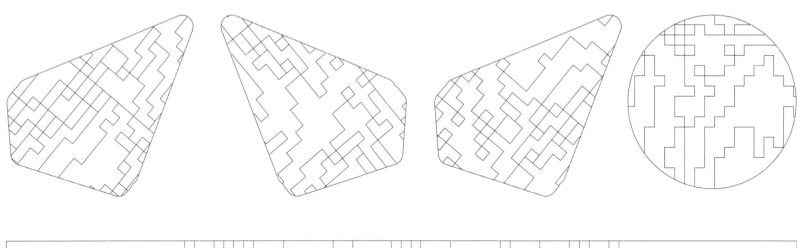

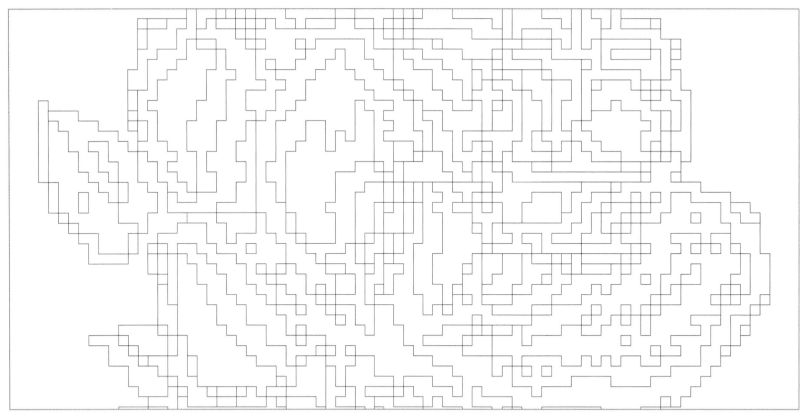

MORE IDEAS AND INFORMATION

• Blue is the obvious choice for the backing paper, but of course you can use any colour.

• You could choose colours for the sky that make it look serene or stormy.

• Raise the boats at the front of the picture with sticky pads to give a 3D effect.

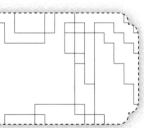

Seven Folded Stars

Incredibly simple to make once you get the knack, these stars are created from a single triangle and a few folds. They're very versatile – just use your imagination – and you could even make them twinkle with a touch of glitter.

MATERIALS AND TOOLS

- Needle and thread

INSTRUCTIONS

1 To make one star, colour it in as marked and cut it out

2 With the side with blank areas facing upwards, fold one of the larger triangles forwards along the fold line and then fold the smaller triangle backwards along the fold line. Do the same with the other two larger triangles.

3 There will be one complete triangle visible on the star. Fold one corner of this under one of the part triangles next to it, to hold the folds in place.

4 Using the needle and thread, sew through one of the thicker points to make a loop for hanging the star.

5 The process is the same for the other stars.

MORE IDEAS AND INFORMATION

• Colour the stars in festive colours – red, green and gold, for instance – and hang them on the Christmas tree.

• Or you could opt to colour each one in shades of a different rainbow hue.

• You could also link these stars together to make a short garland or use them for a mobile.

Floral Alphabet

These letters are an incredibly useful resource for your crafting. Personalise a picture or product with an initial or a name, or spell out a complete phrase. All you need to do is colour them and cut them out.

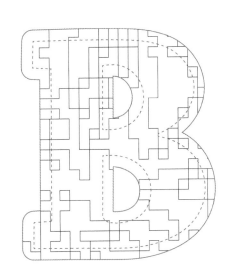

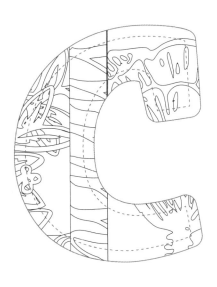

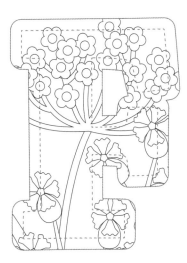

MORE IDEAS AND INFORMATION

- Label party balloons with children's initials. They'll be so charmed they won't demand a different colour (hopefully!).

- Paint four jars, stick a letter to each one – H, O, M and E for example – and fill with fresh flowers.

- Make the owner's initial the centrepiece of a beautiful bookplate for a volume that's treasured.

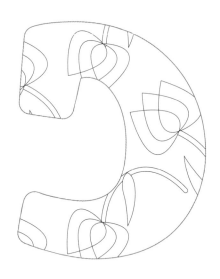

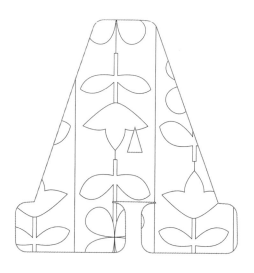

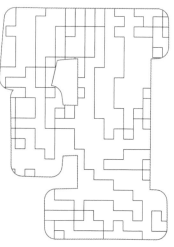